OCT 2006

P9-DEL-641
7930282

APPLEGATE LIBRARY

Placer County Library
350 Nevada Street
Auburn, CA 95603

YOUR PICTURE HERE
WISH
MAKE FRIENDS MAKE THINGS MAKE MAGIC MAKE Believe!

TO: violET 4U

FROM:

FAIRY DUST

Fairies believe that wishing is a magical way of making good things happen, because wishing makes us feel good.

WHAT YOU NEED

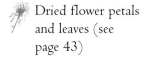

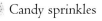

- Dried flower petals and leaves (see page 43)
- Sequins
- Birdseed
- Candy sprinkles
- Colored sand (from a craft store, or add food coloring to clean sand)
- Colored confetti paper
- Colored glitter

For thousands of years Fairy Dust was made only by fairies, but now you can make it, too.

WHAT YOU DO

1. Carefully mix any or all of the things listed at left.
2. When you feel love and kindness in your heart, you know your Fairy Dust is ready!
3. To use your Fairy Dust, take a tiny pinch and hold it over your heart. Close your eyes and make a wish. Finish your wish by sprinkling the dust around you and thanking the fairies for their help.

FAIRY DUST HOLDER

After you make your Fairy Dust, create a special little bag or box to store it.

WHAT YOU DO

- Use a small plastic bag or brown paper bag tied with a ribbon.
- Cover an empty bandage box with fancy Con-Tact paper.
- Make a little bag out of any material or fabric (see Potpourri Bag, page 46, for instructions).
- Use tacky glue (it dries quickly) to decorate your holder with beads, jewels, glitter, sequins, etc.

Knock, knock.

Who's there?

Wilma.

Wilma who?

Will my wishes come true?

WISH MAKERS

Every time you make a wish, you're making fairy magic!

You don't really have to wish on anything special to make your wish come true, but it sure is fun when you do. Here are some fun things to wish upon:

- **The first star you see at night**—Close and open your eyes quickly. The first star you see is the one to wish on.
- **A white horse**—You must wink at it three times.
- **A four-leaf clover**—Throw it over your shoulder or put it in your shoe.
- **A dandelion**—You must blow the dandelion head bare with one huge puff.
- **A one-eyed car**—When you see a car with one front headlight out, touch your nose and say, "Wishy-washy."
- **Your favorite stuffed animal**—Kissing its right hind leg will kick your wish into place.
- **Butterfly**—If a butterfly lands on you, whatever wish you make will probably come true.
- **Fairy kisses**—If you can get a fairy to kiss you three times, you will get anything your heart desires as long as you give the fairy three kisses back.

WISH BOX

A wish box is good for keeping all your wishes together.

WHAT YOU DO

1. Cover your box with your decorations, using glue or tape.
2. Cut some plain white paper into small strips.
3. Think about something that would make you really happy if it came true. Then write your wish down on a small slip of paper, using a crayon or pen.
4. Fill your box with all your special wishes. Whenever you feel like it, add more wishes to your box.

WHAT YOU NEED

- Empty tissue box (any size)
- Decorations like buttons, bows, beads, stickers, glitter, or sequins
- Glue or tape
- Scissors
- Plain white paper
- Crayon or pen

SILLY SPELLS

Don't be surprised if you see a beautiful white glow coming from the tip of your wand after you make a wish!

It's also fun to use your magic wand to cast silly spells. You can make up some really crazy ones like these:

Mud pie, mud pie on my plate,
Turn into candy, and don't make me wait!
Or
Earthquakes and bellyaches, swiggles and wiggles,
Hocus-pocus, you've got the giggles!
Or
Warthogs and pollywogs, icicles and Popsicles,
Peppers and pickles, you're going to get the tickles!
Or
Alacazam, big bad trolls are near;
Now it's time to disappear!

Try filling in these spells:

Magic ice and melted snow, ______________________

Goose pie, French fry, ______________________

Doofus, loofus, tinkle and tea, ______________________

____

FAIRY SPELLING BEE

Write the two words "fairy wishes" in big letters on a piece of paper. Cut out each letter from the two words and move them around to see how many words you can make. Write all the words you come up with on the lines below. Each letter may be used again to make new words.

SOME ANSWERS

fair	his	weary	air	wish	fish	is	she	he	airy	her	hers
swish	fishy	rise	wear	yes	sew	fairies	ware	wars	far	says	sir
has	saw	few	fresh	wash	iris	Irish	share	fry	war	say	are

FAIRY BOAT

WHAT YOU NEED

- A walnut shell
- Gummi candy, gumdrop, marshmallow, or some clay
- Small piece of paper or a flower petal
- Scissors
- Markers, colored pencils, or crayons
- Toothpick
- Tacky glue

A fairy boat is a wonderful way to go on magical trips.

WHAT YOU DO

1. Let a grown-up crack open a walnut for you so that there are two neat-looking halves. Eat the nut inside. Mmmm!
2. Stick a little Gummi candy, gumdrop, marshmallow, or clay into the bottom of one half of the shell.
3. Create a sail by cutting out a triangular piece of paper 1½ to 2 inches high and decorate it with crayons, colored pencils, or markers. You can also use a flower petal as your sail.
4. Glue a toothpick to the middle of your paper sail. Let it dry thoroughly. You can also stick your toothpick through the bottom part of your paper or flower petal sail, then bend the sail slightly and push the toothpick through the top.
5. Insert the sail into the candy or clay.
6. Set sail to your walnut shell boat in a creek, puddle, sink, bathtub, or bucket of water.

The Flower Fairy Doll

Today I'll make a fairy friend
With red rose head and iris eye;
Her pretty wings will nicely blend
Sweet colors like a butterfly.

Her hair will curl like dandelions,
To form a crown around her head;
A poppy will be her gown so fine
Of pearly pink and richest red.

I'll dance and play fun games with her,
Until I must slow down and rest;
From dawn to noon to way past supper,
My fairy friend will have the best!

FLOWER FAIRY DOLLS

Fairies use columbines for their shoes and nasturtiums for their hats.

Making fairy dolls from flowers is a cinch because all the materials are naturally found outdoors. You can also ask a florist or plant nursery to give you a few old blossoms. Silk flowers will do the trick, too! Here are a few wonderful ways to make your own flower fairy dolls.

WHAT YOU DO

- **Flower doll body**—Use a stick pin to make small pinholes in two sides of a Canterbury bell, foxglove, petunia, hollyhock, day lily, trumpet, or fuchsia. Insert a stem or twig through the holes to serve as your doll's arms. The petals will be a fancy skirt and two stamens can be left in place for her legs.

- **Flower doll head**—Break off the stem from an old, wilted rose. Pick off all the loose petals and what you will have left is a small, round little bud with a face ready for some makeup. Now take colored markers to draw eyes, nose, and a mouth. You can also use a cherry tomato for your doll's head. Stick a toothpick into the head and insert it into the doll's body.

- **Pansy dolls**—Fold a pansy leaf around the stem of a pansy like a cape. Poke a tiny twig through the leaf to help keep the cape on and to create two arms. You can also fold any leaf in half, and with your fingernail, make a small slit or head hole in the middle of the folded leaf. When you stick a pansy on a stem into the hole, you'll have a flower doll.

- Accessorize your flower doll. For a cute little hat, bend a green leaf over the head and pin it with a piece of toothpick or a tiny twig. Make a cloak out of another leaf. With a needle and thread, string a dainty necklace of tiny pink clovers. Add a ribbon for a bow tie or a cute curly blouse. Give her hair by splitting some dandelion stems, dipping them in water, and gently pulling on them. They will curl up ever so nicely.

OTHER IDEAS

- Make a ballerina doll using a crabapple for the head, twig and grasses for the upper body, a mushroom for the skirt, and twigs for legs.

FAIRY HOUSE

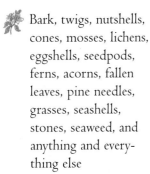

What could be more exciting to build than a tiny house and furniture made from twigs, mosses, ferns, and flowers? You would make the fairies so happy. You can build a fairy house just about anywhere with just about anything. No two fairy homes look exactly alike. So have fun building one in your own special way.

WHAT YOU NEED

- Bark, twigs, nutshells, cones, mosses, lichens, eggshells, seedpods, ferns, acorns, fallen leaves, pine needles, grasses, seashells, stones, seaweed, and anything and everything else
- Tacky glue

WHAT YOU DO

1. Choose a special spot where you can build your fairy house, like a beautiful but secret place in your garden, under a tree in the woods, on a piece of beach driftwood, hidden in a little drawer in your bedroom, on your windowsill, or even in the corner of your closet.
2. Clean the ground or area around where you plan to build your fairy house, and lay out all the building materials you have gathered together.
3. Decide what you will need for the walls, ceiling, roof, tables, chairs, and so on. You can use twigs for the walls, a piece of bark for the roof, a flat stone for the floor. Experiment! If you want to be able to move your fairy house around, you may want to assemble it on a piece of heavy cardboard or a thin piece of wood.

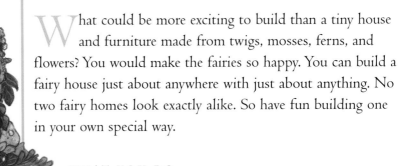

- Build a bed out of walnut halves and add leaves, flower blossoms, moss, seaweed, or even lettuce to make it soft and cozy.
- Find some fabric scraps and lay them down for carpeting.
- Recycle used gift wrap or pieces of spare wallpaper to cover the walls. (Ask a decorating store to give you an old wallpaper sample book.)
- Cut out tiny pictures from magazines and catalogues to hang as paintings on the walls.
- Make a mirror by gluing a small piece of aluminum foil to cardboard.
- Use leaves or small fern fronds as place mats or a tablecloth for your table. Or turn fabric scraps or colored facial tissue into tablecloths, bedding, and curtains.
- Cracked nutshells or tiny seashells make great bowls, cups, platters, and dishes. So do bottle caps, thimbles, jar lids, and small plastic tubs. Use seeds, berries, or Play-Doh for pretend food.
- Fill a bottle cap with clay or chewing gum and cover with moss or green tissue paper. Stick a tiny twig with green leaves into the clay or gum and you have an easy-to-care-for houseplant. You can also add plants, trees, and gardens using pictures cut out from magazines.

In your mind a wish can start, and it'll come true in your fairy heart!

FAIRY CROWNS

Fairy crowns are lovely to look at and so regal to wear. They can be decorated with real, silk, or dried flowers, sequins, glitter, metallic stars, or anything else.

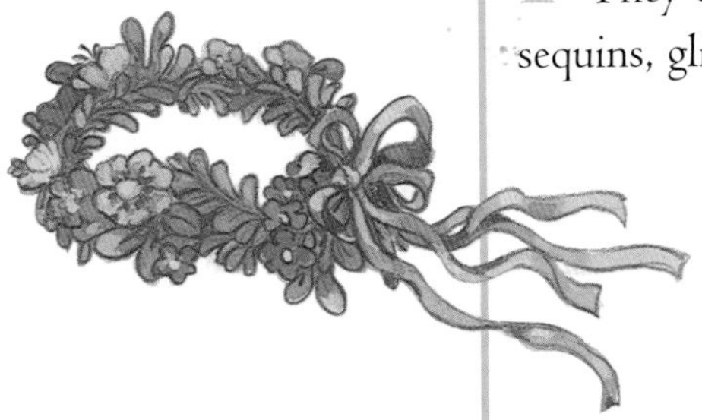

WHAT YOU NEED

- Fresh flowers
- Wire or cloth headband
- Ribbons
- Thin branches

FRESH FLOWER CROWN

WHAT YOU DO

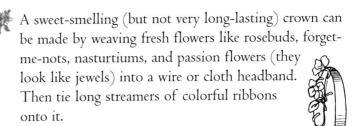

- A sweet-smelling (but not very long-lasting) crown can be made by weaving fresh flowers like rosebuds, forget-me-nots, nasturtiums, and passion flowers (they look like jewels) into a wire or cloth headband. Then tie long streamers of colorful ribbons onto it.

- You can also braid together thin branches of willow, bay, or fern in a circle large enough to fit around your head. Add flowers by weaving their stems in and out of the base. Long ribbons can be tied on to help hold your crown together and to add a touch of color.

DRIED OR SILK FLOWER CROWN

WHAT YOU DO

1. Fit floral wire around the top of your head and then twist the ends together to make a comfortable fit. Snip off any excess wire.
2. Starting at the twisted ends, add a flower or leaf. Attach it to your crown using a small strip of thin wire or green floral tape. Add the next flower and wind the tape or wire around, repeating the process until your crown is covered with flowers.
3. Twist a strip of thin wire around one end of each ribbon and then attach it to your crown. Use a bow or a flower to hide where the ribbon meets the crown.
4. Cut the ends of the ribbons at an angle or at different lengths to make your crown more interesting-looking. You can also add metallic stars or strips, netting, glitter, tinsel, beads, and the like.

WHAT YOU NEED

- Thick covered floral wire (from a craft or floral shop)
- Scissors or wire cutters
- Assorted silk or dried flowers and leaves
- Thin wire or green floral tape cut into 4-inch strips
- 6-to-10-inch pieces of colored ribbons

MAGIC DISGUISES

Magic happens when you use a pinch of love, a bit of luck, and a lot of kindness.

Every now and then it's fun to hide under masks, wigs, mustaches, beards, glasses, or false noses. When you are walking along with a fairy friend, try on a fern mustache or a leaf mask.

WHAT YOU DO

1. Look for big leaves, soft branches, vines, or anything else that you can comfortably hold to your face.
2. Carefully thread pieces of ribbon or a large rubber band through the edges of your disguise so that you can wear it around your head. Or glue, tape, or staple your mask onto a stick or twig so you can hold it up to your face.
3. You can make costumes for their giggle effect, or you can hold a contest and award titles for the best mask, the funniest one, the prettiest one, and so on.

FAIRY CLOTHES

Dressing up like a fairy is always fun.

WHAT YOU NEED

- Pretty pieces of old fabric, aprons, or scarves
- Glitter, sequins, ribbons, beads, gemstones, or leaves
- Tacky glue

WHAT YOU DO

1. You can decorate a piece of scrap fabric with glitter, sequins, or ribbons to give it that fairyish look and then tie or pin it around your shoulders, waist, or chest.
2. Or with your mom's permission, glue shiny things onto two old aprons and tie them around your waist, one in front and one in back, to cover yourself completely.
3. Make a quick leaf skirt by pinning large green leaves to a big old scarf with safety pins. Then tie the scarf around your waist.
4. You can also tie the ends of a few flowing scarves to a belt and then wear the belt.

FAIRY WINGS

WHAT YOU NEED

- A big piece of heavy construction paper, poster board, or cardboard (or you can tape or glue two smaller pieces together)
- Pencil
- Scissors
- Two strips of ribbon, 14 to 16 inches long
- Crayons, markers, or paint
- Tape or tacky glue
- Glitter, gemstones, sequins, stickers, feathers, etc.

You cannot pretend to be a fairy unless you have your own set of wings. These directions will guarantee a smooth flight wherever your wings may take you.

WHAT YOU DO

1. Use the pattern at the lower left to give you a good idea of the shape you need for your fairy wings. Fold your construction paper or cardboard in half lengthwise. Draw a wing shape directly on the paper, making sure it's the right size wing for you. A good wing size is about 16 to 18 inches high by 10 to 12 inches wide.

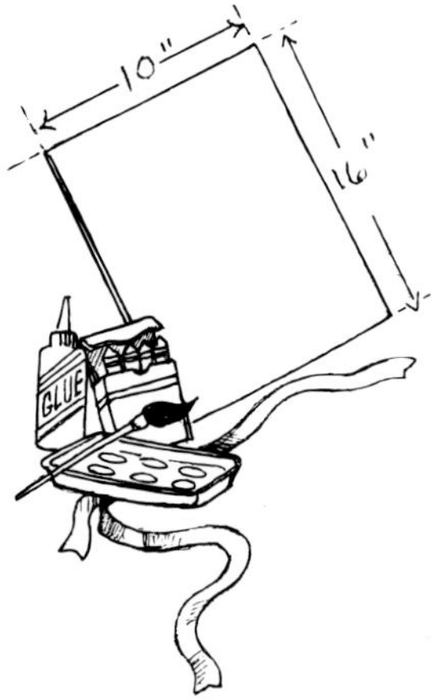

2. Cut out your folded wings and open them flat, or staple or glue two wing pieces together.
3. Make two little holes in each wing above and below where your shoulders will be when you put the wings on (see the illustration).

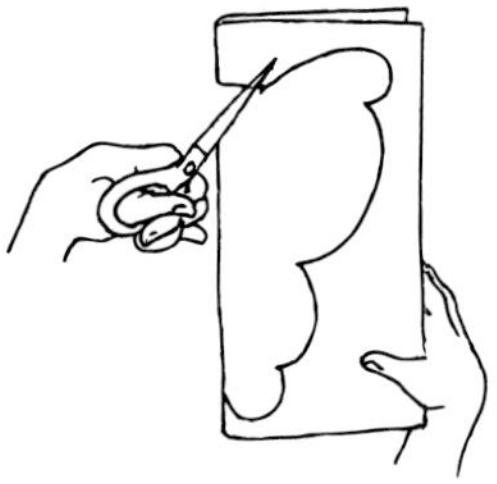

4. Thread the ribbons through the holes, tie them together, and knot them. Allow plenty of room for your arms and shoulders to fit comfortably through the ribbons.

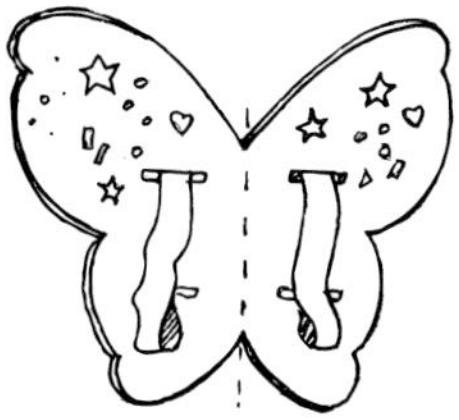

5. Decorate your fairy wings by drawing wonderful patterns on them or by gluing on bits of colored, sparkly things. When your wings are completely dry, put them on, and off you'll fly!

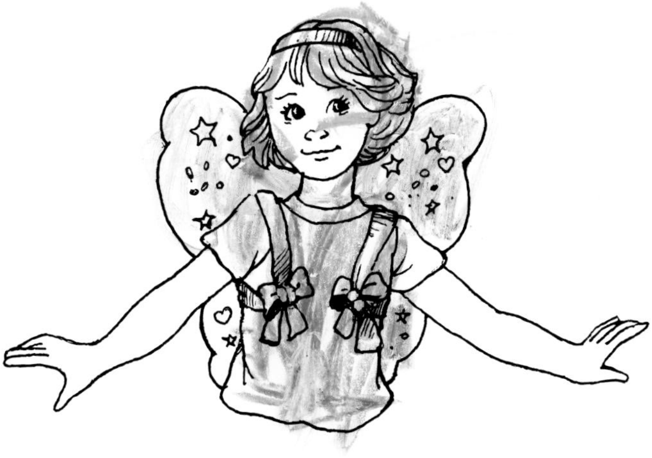

Wings and a dream can take you anywhere!

FAIRY JEWELRY

Fairies believe that whenever a rainbow touches the ground, the bright colors give birth to flowers!

It's easy to design your own nature jewelry, when you know where to look.

FRESH FLOWER NECKLACE

WHAT YOU DO

1. Remove leaves from wildflowers like daisies, Queen Anne's lace, black-eyed Susans, or violets. Cut the stems to 3 inches long.
2. Make a small slit with your fingernail through the middle of a flower stem. Stick another flower stem through the slit of your first stem and pull it all the way through.
3. Make a slit in the second stem and slide a third flower through that slit. Continue until you have the length you wish (see the illustration).
4. To form a circle, either tie two stems together or work the stem of the last flower gently into the slit on the very first flower. Wildflower necklaces are delicate, so remember to make your necklace big enough to slip over your head without breaking.

OTHER IDEAS

- You can also thread a big needle with thick thread or light cord (1 to 2 feet long) and tie a knot at one end. With your needle, sew right through the thickest part of any flower. Keep adding flowers until the cord has enough flowers to comfortably fit around your neck. Tie a knot at the other end. Then tie a piece of ribbon to each end to make a bow so that you can easily take your necklace on or off.
- Use a needle and thread to string different types of dried melon, squash, or pumpkin seeds into a necklace. Keep your necklace its own natural color, or paint the seeds with tempera poster paints. You can also add buttons, colored tissue paper, and pieces of colored pipe cleaners or drinking straws for a unique necklace.
- To make a bracelet, use a long, thick-stemmed flower like a hibiscus, daisy, or poppy. Cut off as long a stem as possible and slit the stem up the middle, almost up to the point where the blossom begins. Tie or twist the two ends gently around your wrist and wear it with the blossom in front.
- Small rings can be made from violets, pansies, and other small flowers. Leave some stem, and cut a small slit at the point where the stem joins the flower and then slip the tip of the stem through the slit.
- Make pins, barrettes, and hair combs by tacky-gluing dried or silk flowers, buttons, seeds, gemstones, or shells onto old jewelry backings, barrettes, and hair combs. Be sure to ask if you can use them first. If you can't, ask to buy some inexpensive ones at a craft shop.

WHAT YOU NEED

- 10 or more pieces of colored facial tissue or tissue paper
- 10 or more pipe cleaners
- Pinking shears (optional)
- 6 to 10 inches of heavy thread
- Needle

PAPER FLOWER NECKLACE

WHAT YOU DO

1. Fold a piece of paper or facial tissue like an accordion, then take a pipe cleaner and twist it around the folded center of the paper flower (see the illustration). Cut off the ends of the pipe cleaner. Repeat for more flowers.

2. While the tissue flower is still folded, cut the ends with a pinking shears. If you don't have pinking shears, open up the tissue petals and gently tear their edges to make a scalloped look.

3. Cut a piece of heavy thread long enough to fit loosely around your neck. Thread a needle with the thread and tie the end into a knot. Sew through the center of each flower with your needle and thread. Make more tissue flowers as you need them to create a necklace.

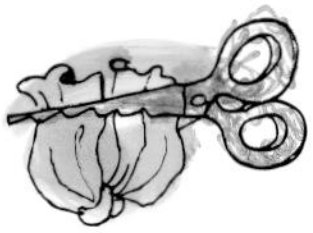

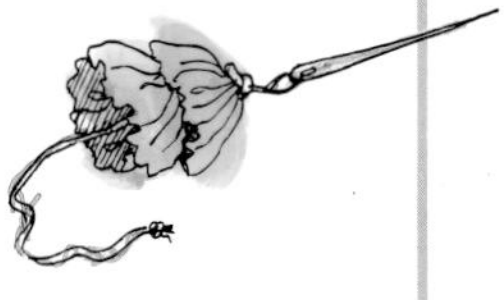

4. When your necklace looks full enough, tie the two ends of the thread together to form your necklace.
5. Paper flowers can also be used for other things like flower baskets, crowns, party decorations, and presents. Add a wire or pipe cleaner stem and you can slip them into a bouquet or vase.

S P E C I A L   E A R R I N G S

WHAT YOU DO

- In the spring when maple trees begin dropping their seeds, gather a few of the pods while they are still green. Gently pry open the full seed ends and attach them to your earlobes for some wonderful earrings. (You can also split the seed ends and stick them on the bridge of your nose and pretend they are glasses.)

- Take a couple of "snaps" from a tall stalk of snapdragons and use them as clip-on earrings.

- Hang connected cherries over your ears for some delicious dangly earrings.

Stars are diamonds in the sky. Your wishes make them sparkle and fly!

FUN FAIRY MAKEUP

Rainbows make people stop and smile. That's why fairies always look for them!

You can make your own fairy makeup, using natural ingredients.

WHAT YOU DO

- Rub sweet-smelling rose petals all over your skin to create a fantastically fragrant perfume that will last for hours.
- Loosely fill a small, clean glass jar to the top with some scented rose petals. Then add water, screw on the lid very tightly, shake, and let settle for three to four weeks. Strain into a bowl covered with a piece of cheesecloth, and carefully pour the perfume through a funnel into an empty perfume bottle. Finish with a pretty bow to make a delightful gift!
- Make nail polish by cutting flower petals to fit your fingernails. Lay a petal over your nail, then take a small paintbrush and dip it into a little cup of water. Brush the "water polish" over the petal on your nail. (My, what long nails you have, my dear!)
- Create your own makeup by pouring a little strawberry, cranberry, blueberry, or other berry juice into a small paper cup. Dip a clean paintbrush into the berry juice cup and paint your cheeks and lips.

INSTANT RAINBOW

Perform this trick on a nice sunny day and you will get the brightest rainbow.

WHAT YOU DO

1. Choose a room with a window opposite a big white wall.
2. Fill a small bowl with water and place it on the window's ledge or on a table next to the bowl.
3. Set a small mirror next to the dish.
4. Tell your audience you will make a rainbow appear from nowhere.
5. Take your mirror and place it in the water while holding it at an angle to capture the sunshine and flash it onto the white wall.
6. Point your magic wand at the wall and say, "Abracadabra! It's fairy clear. A rainbow will soon appear!"

WHAT YOU NEED

- Small bowl
- Small mirror
- Sunshine
- Magic wand

Magic Garden Recipe

If your garden starts to droop,
Mix a cup of magic soup;
Before your flowers drink it up,
Add fairy wishes to the cup!

RAINBOW FLOWERS

You can grow your own rainbow right in your own yard.

WHAT YOU DO

1. Choose an area of ground—any size over 12 inches will do. Or plant your rainbow in a large metal pan or pot and place it by a sunny window.
2. Turn over the soil really well and add some fertilizer.
3. Trace out the pattern of a rainbow arch with a stick or hoe. You can even add the shape of a pot of gold at the end of your rainbow.
4. Go to a plant nursery and choose small flowers in the colors of the rainbow: red, orange, yellow, green, blue, indigo, and violet.
5. Plant the taller blossoms in the back and the shorter ones up front. Use yellow marigolds or poppies for your pot of gold at one end. At the other end of the rainbow, plant a patch of low-growing greenery like chamomile, thyme, or grass for the fairies to dance on and hold their fairy meetings.
6. Water often and early in the morning. Take your time and give them a long, deep, gentle drink. Think about how you would like to be treated if you were a plant or flower.
7. One night, take your flashlight out and be the first person to see a rainbow in the dark!

WHAT YOU NEED

- 12 inches or more of garden space or a large pan or pot filled with dirt
- Small bag of fertilizer
- Stick or hoe
- A variety of flowers and plants

FAIRY GARDEN BASKET

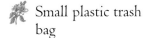

WHAT YOU NEED

- Small plastic trash bag
- Scissors
- Basket, any size or shape
- Small bag of rich potting soil
- Flowers like pansies and zinnias; plants like thyme and moss

It's simple to create a tiny enchanted fairy garden in a basket.

WHAT YOU DO

1. Cut a small plastic trash bag in half. Use it as a liner for your basket, making sure it completely covers the bottom and sides of the basket.
2. Fill your basket with good, rich potting soil. Be sure to bring the soil up almost to the edge of the plastic inside your basket.
3. Plant your basket with flowers and plants that fairies love, like pansies and thyme, or choose your own favorites.
4. Finish by tucking some moss and lichens around the plants to form a fairy carpet.
5. You can build and furnish a tiny fairy house for your basket. Look on page 22 to see how.
6. Set your basket in a cool, brightly lit spot. Water the soil only when it is dry, but mist the plants with a spray bottle to keep them looking good.

SCRAMBLED WORDS

The pixies have mixed up some words and can't seem to get them back together again. Can you unscramble them and see what they spell? Use the words listed below as a guide. Good luck!

WORDS

wand lily dream crystal sprite
magic believe firefly elves happiness

1. VELES ____________
2. TLCRYSA ____________
3. CIMAG ____________
4. TESPRI ____________
5. EVBELIE ____________
6. FLYEFIR ____________
7. IYLL ____________
8. NWDA ____________
9. MDRAE ____________
10. NHAPISEPS ____________

SCRAMBLED WORDS ANSWERS:

1. elves 2. crystal 3. magic 4. sprite 5. believe 6. firefly 7. lily 8. wand 9. dream 10. happiness

THE MAGIC FLOWER

At the end of the rainbow, before you reach the pot of gold, there are seven big pots filled with beautiful colors that the fairies use to paint the flowers, fruits, and foliage.

Here is a trick that lets you transform a white rose or carnation into one that is half white and half green!

WHAT YOU DO

1. Cut the stem of a white flower down the middle lengthwise.
2. Put one half of the stem in a glass of water and the other half in a glass of water mixed with green food coloring.
3. A few hours later, exactly half the flower will turn green! The flower will suck up the water through tiny tubes in its stem. Half the stem will suck up clear water, and the other half will drink the colored water. It works just as well with other flowers and other colors. This flower makes a great birthday present as well as a magic trick.

DRIED FLOWERS

Want to know how the fairies keep their blossoms alive forever? They dry them! Then they use them for all kinds of things like bouquets, potpourris, centerpieces, sculptures, decorations, and garlands.

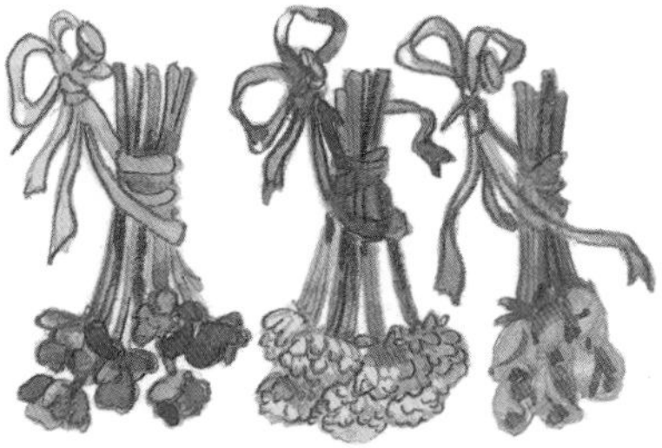

WHAT YOU DO

1. Trim the flower stems to different lengths. Bunch about six stems together, making sure the flowers don't rub against one another.
2. Hold the bunch together with the rubber band, then tie a ribbon around the rubber band.
3. Hang the bouquet upside down from a beam, over a window, or on a wall—as long as it's not in direct sunlight. When the scent fades, spray it with a little perfume to liven it up.

WHAT YOU NEED

- Sweet-smelling flowers like cosmos, roses, larkspurs, or daisies and sweet-smelling flowering herbs like sage, yarrow, thyme, and lavender. Colors change as flowers dry; yellow and orange flowers keep their color best.
- Rubber band
- Ribbon

ROSE DROPS

WHAT YOU NEED

- Needle and thread
- 10 to 20 rosebuds, either fresh or dried
- Rose petals and green leaves
- Pearls, beads, and other jewels (optional)
- Small piece of ribbon

Rose drops are lovely to smell as well as to see. They can be hung over your bed, in your window, on a wall, in a tree—even around your neck!

WHAT YOU DO

1. Thread a needle and knot it at the end. You can make the thread as long as you want.
2. Carefully insert your threaded needle through the center of a fresh or dried rosebud (or rose petal). Gently pull the rosebud down to the bottom of your knotted thread so that the flower doesn't break off.
3. String three rosebuds, then string a leaf or a petal. You can also add pearls, beads, or other jewels in between the roses and leaves. Have fun making up your own designs. When it's long enough, knot the other end of the thread.
4. When you're ready to hang your rose drop chain, tie a small piece of ribbon tightly around one of the knotted ends of your thread. Make a pretty bow with the rest of the ribbon, leaving a little loop so that you can hang it (see the illustration).

POTPOURRI

What is one of the most wonderful things about the outdoors? It smells so fresh and sweet. You can bring some of that outdoor goodness inside with potpourri (pronounced poe-poo-ree).

WHAT YOU DO

1. Gather some flower blossoms with different colors and scents.
2. Pull apart the blossoms. Throw away everything but the petals and some leaves (or ask your local florist for some wilted or discarded flowers).
3. Place the petals on a metal cookie sheet or tray to dry for a few days, away from sunlight. Turn the petals over once a day.
4. When they're completely dry, sprinkle the petals with a spoonful of mixed spices or dried herbs and a few drops of essential oil.
5. Mix the dry petals and herbs gently with your hands.
6. Scoop them into a clean, airtight jar.
7. Paint the lid and tie a ribbon around the jar to make a special gift or decoration.
8. To use potpourri, be sure to keep the lid closed until you want your room to smell good; then open the top for a little while. To keep the nice smell, add several drops of potpourri oil every few months.

WHAT YOU NEED

- Sweet-smelling flowers like roses, lavender, geraniums, and violets
- Cookie sheet or metal tray
- 1 tablespoon mixed spices like cloves, cinnamon, nutmeg, or allspice and/or 1 tablespoon dried herbs like rosemary, marjoram, mint, sage, or thyme
- A few drops of potpourri oils, found in drug, craft, and beauty supply stores
- Glass jar (baby food jars work nicely)
- Paint
- Ribbons

POTPOURRI BAG, PURSE, AND PILLOW

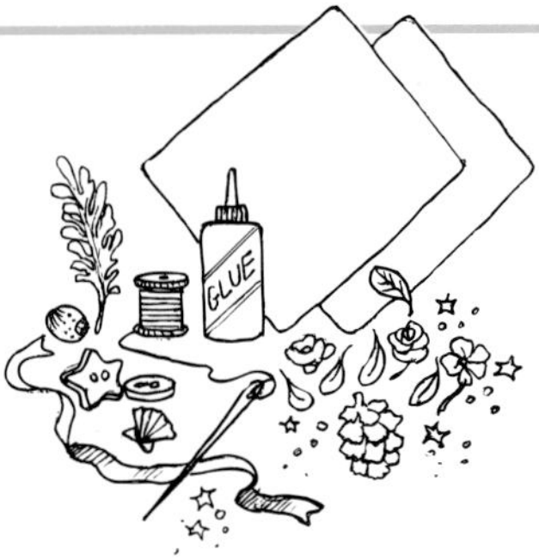

WHAT YOU NEED

- A big handful of potpourri
- One or two 6-inch squares of fabric
- Small rubber band
- 6-inch length of ribbon
- Scissors
- Small piece of Velcro or a button (optional)
- Decorations like lace, ribbons, sequins, beads, jewels, etc.
- 36-inch cord

Another way to save potpourri, especially if you are going to give it as a gift, is to put it into a pretty nylon net bag, felt purse, or fabric pillow.

TO MAKE A BAG

WHAT YOU DO

1. Lay one fabric square on a flat surface and spoon about 2 tablespoons of your dried potpourri mixture in the middle.
2. Gather all four ends of the square to the center and slip a rubber band around the top. Double or triple it if necessary until it's tight.
3. Tightly tie a pretty ribbon around the rubber band.

TO MAKE A PURSE

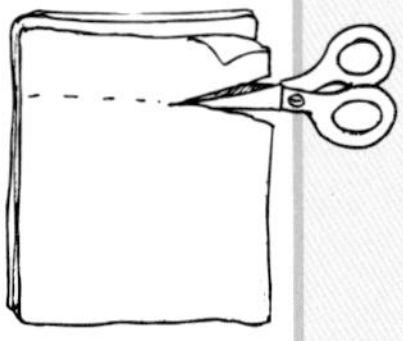

WHAT YOU DO

1. Take two 6-inch square pieces of fabric. Cut 2 inches off the top of one of the pieces.
2. Lay the smaller piece over the full piece. When you bend the full bottom piece over the short top piece, it will give you a little

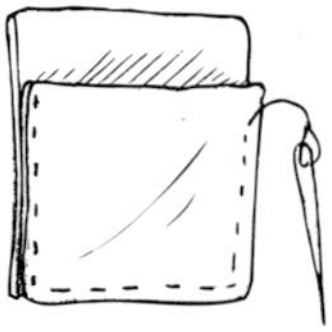

flap (see the illustration). You can glue on small pieces of Velcro or sew on a button and cut out a hole to help the flap cover your purse.

3. Glue or stitch around the side edges where the two layers meet, leaving the top part open.

4. Glue or stitch a 36-inch cord to the top corners of your purse.
5. Decorate your purse with beads, jewels, or other sparkly things.
6. Add your potpourri or Fairy Dust.

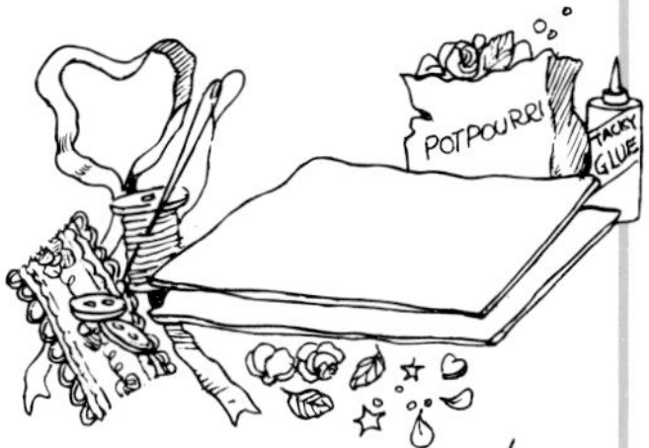

TO MAKE A PILLOW

WHAT YOU DO

1. Take two 6-inch squares of fabric.
2. With the right sides of the fabric facing each other (so it looks inside out), sew the pillow together around the edges, leaving one side open about $\frac{1}{4}$ inch for turning and filling (see the illustration).

3. Turn the square right side out and gently fill it with 1 cup potpourri.
4. Sew the opening closed with tiny stitches.
5. You can decorate the pillow by gluing or sewing on lace, ribbon, sequins, etc.

Believing creates magic, and magic has power!

Fairy Rings

Whenever you find a fairy ring,
You can be sure that sprites are near;
We love to dance and sing and play,
Until the moonlight shines so clear.

We search the world for many things,
Like mushrooms, moss, and pretty flowers;
We use them all to make our rings,
And have such fun through darkest hours.

When in the fields the day you spend,
Walk soft and gently, oh, please do;
You'll always be a fairy friend
And we will be so kind to you!

FAIRY RING

If you want to create a little place where the fairies can dance on moonlit nights, try making your own version of a fairy ring.

WHAT YOU NEED

- Rocks, pebbles, twigs, flowers
- Saucer
- Water

WHAT YOU DO

1. Gather rocks, pebbles, twigs, or flowers.
2. Place them in a circle in a beautiful spot.
3. Set a water-filled saucer nearby to reflect the moonlight and to help attract other small creatures. Be sure to keep the water fresh!

OTHER IDEAS

- Create a bigger fairy ring by planting sunflowers in a large circle. When the flowers grow tall and bloom, you'll have your own fairy hideaway for when you want to be alone. You can also turn it into a sunflower fun house where you can entertain your fairy friends.

Some mushrooms grow in circles, but they aren't really fairy rings—it's just that they spread their tiny seeds (called spores) in circles.

PRESSED FLOWERS

WHAT YOU NEED

- Flowers like anemones, marigolds, pansies, and baby's breath
- Plant material like ferns, mosses, leaves, and seed heads
- Newspaper
- Tweezers
- Tape
- Heavy book like a phone directory
- White glue

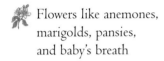

Whether you live in the city, in the country, or by the sea, you are sure to find some flowers, leaves, and other plant material that you can gather and press for your flower pictures. Pressing flowers is simple yet gives you the opportunity to be very artistic. You can create so many fancy things like note cards, stationery, decorative gift boxes, and bookmarks.

WHAT YOU DO

1. Gather some fresh flowers, leaves, or other plants. Collect flowers during dry weather or after any dew has evaporated, or else your flowers will turn brown when pressed. Use buds, partially opened blooms, full blossoms, and leaves.
2. Spread a piece of newspaper over a hard, flat surface and arrange your plants, leaves, and flowers on it. Make sure to arrange the flowers on the newspaper in the final form you would like to see them. Tweezers will help. Try bending, curving, and shaping the blossoms to make them as pretty as possible. Put a piece of tape over the stems to secure them in place.
3. Cover the flowers with another piece of newspaper and place a heavy book over the flowers to keep them pressed down for about two weeks.

PRESSED FLOWER PICTURE

Create a beautiful design by thinking about how pretty the flowers look in a field or garden. That will help you arrange them in a very natural way.

WHAT YOU DO

1. Gently lift your pressed flowers off the newspaper with tweezers.
2. Lay them on a piece of poster board or heavy paper. Move them around until you come up with a design you like, then glue them down. You can also glue on other flat objects like paper doilies, fabric, etc.
3. Finish your creation by laying ribbon or lace around the edges or slip your board into a picture frame.

FAIRY FLASH!

Before helping yourself to any flowers or plants, be polite and ask permission first. If the flowers you want to use are wild, find out if they are protected or endangered before you pick them. Instead of pulling the flowers up by their roots, use scissors to cut them. That way they will have a chance to bloom again.

WHAT YOU NEED

- Pressed flowers, leaves, plants
- Tweezers
- Poster board or heavy paper
- Glue
- Paper doilies, netting, fabric, ribbon, trim (optional)
- Frame (optional)

FLOWER BOOKMARK

WHAT YOU NEED

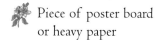

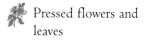

- Piece of poster board or heavy paper
- Scissors
- Colored marking pens
- Pressed flowers and leaves
- Glue
- Tweezers
- Piece of transparent film cover with adhesive backing (found in craft stores)

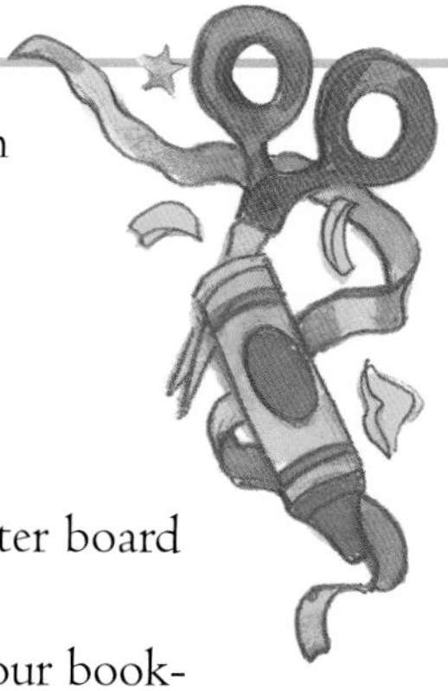

You can also make a bookmark with pressed flowers. For a special gift, write a friendly greeting on it.

WHAT YOU DO

1. Cut a 3-by-6-inch strip from the poster board or heavy paper.
2. Sign your name on the back side of your bookmark or write a birthday or other message with colored marking pens.
3. Use tweezers to lay your flowers and leaves onto the front of your bookmark. When you have arranged a design you like, carefully glue them on. Let dry.
4. Peel off the backing from the transparent film cover and carefully lay the sticky side of the paper over the flower-covered front of your bookmark. This will cover the delicate flowers and protect them from becoming brittle and breaking off while the bookmark is being used.
5. Trim off any extra transparent paper and your bookmark is ready to use.

FAIRY STICK PUPPET

Fairy puppets are fun to create and even more fun to play with. Make a few and put on your own puppet show.

WHAT YOU DO

1. Copy the fairy pattern (see the illustration) on paper or cardboard.
2. Cut it out like you would a paper doll.
3. Decorate with markers, tempera paints, food paint (see page 59), or colored pencils.
4. Your fairy's hair can be cut from yarn, moss, or curled paper strips. Her wings can sparkle with glitter. Her dress can be decorated with flowers and leaves, dried seeds, beans, buttons, matchsticks, pine needles, string, or almost anything else.
5. Glue or tape all your decorations onto your paper fairy to create designs and patterns. When dry, tape or glue your fairy puppet to the Popsicle stick. Wait an hour for your fairy to completely dry and it will be show time!

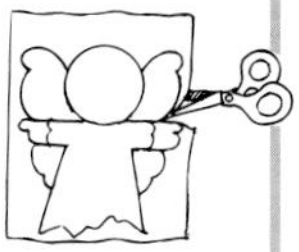

WHAT YOU NEED

- Cardboard or heavy construction paper
- Scissors
- Markers, tempera or food paints, colored pencils
- Decorations like pressed flowers, yarn, glitter, colored tissue paper, etc.
- Glue or tape
- Popsicle stick, paint stirring stick, or long twig

The Practical Fairy

Fairies are practical, they use what they've found
From air, land, and sea, the whole world around;
They waste almost nothing and always recycle
Cans, bottles, and paper, and even old cycles.

They use flower petals from a wilted periwinkle
As brushes to paint sparkling colors that twinkle;
They make umbrellas from mushrooms and flowers,
To keep themselves dry from heavy rain showers.

They make their sailboats from old walnut shells,
Their meetings are opened with Canterbury bells,
Their skirts are made from pretty flowers and leaves,
But it's only their hearts that they wear on their sleeves.

RAINBOW GLASSES

When you hold these rainbow glasses up to your eyes, you'll look at life in a whole new way.

WHAT YOU NEED

- Paper plate or piece of cardboard
- Pencil
- Scissors
- Paints or crayons
- White craft glue or tape
- Colored cellophane or transparent film
- Wooden craft stick
- Decorations like glitter, beads, sequins, etc. (optional)

WHAT YOU DO

1. Fold your paper plate or cardboard in half. Draw your glasses on the paper. They can take the shape of stars, circles, or other designs (see the illustration).
2. Cut out the glasses.
3. Lay your glasses over your eyes to get an idea of where you should cut out holes for your eyes. Take a pencil and lightly mark where your eyeholes should be. Let a grown-up help you cut out the eyeholes so that you can see out perfectly.
4. Paint or color the front of the glasses and let dry.
5. Glue or tape small pieces of cellophane over your eyeholes from the back side of the plate.
6. Glue or tape a wooden craft stick to the side of your paper glasses to use as a holder.
7. If you want to make extra fancy glasses, glue on some sparkly decorations.

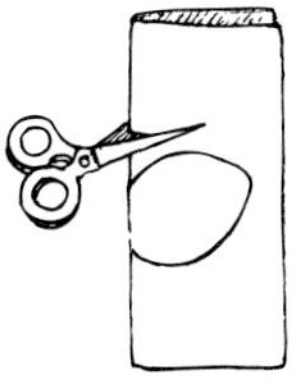

SURPRISE FAIRY GIFTS

Each day is a gift to you.
Make it blossom and grow
into a thing of beauty!

Not every gift has to be bought, wrapped, and tied with a ribbon. Here are some special fairy presents for someone you love.

WHAT YOU DO

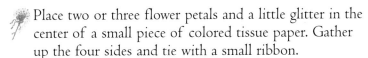

- Place two or three flower petals and a little glitter in the center of a small piece of colored tissue paper. Gather up the four sides and tie with a small ribbon.
- Use a marker to draw a heart and your name on a balloon that you've blown up. Hide it in your mom's or dad's closet as a great surprise.
- Draw some happy faces on a few flower petals and then hide them in a friend's book or bag.
- Pick some beautiful wildflowers, bake some cookies, or pop some popcorn and put them into small baskets to give to friends and neighbors.
- Give a kind word, a big smile, a favor, a bear hug, or a major promise to someone special.

What other gifts do you like to be given that are not bought or wrapped?

FANTASY SUN CATCHER

This simple-to-make bag catches the rays from the sun in the most fantastical way.

WHAT YOU DO

1. Lay the plastic bag flat on top of one piece of aluminum foil or one paper bag.
2. Carefully slide your special things into the plastic bag. Leave some space between the items to allow light to shine through, and so the plastic will stick together.
3. Place the other piece of foil or paper bag on top. Then press it with a warm iron. (Ask a grown-up for some help with this!)
4. Peel away the foil or bags. Trim the plastic into a special shape, if you like.
5. Poke a hole at the top of your magical bag. Slide the ribbon through and make a little loop. Then hang it in a window and watch as the sun dances through it.

OTHER IDEAS

- Use wax paper instead of plastic bags.
- Try adding a little grated crayon or powdered chalk.
- Add cut-up greeting cards or small pieces of colored construction paper or wrapping paper.

WHAT YOU NEED

- Plastic sandwich bag
- 2 pieces of aluminum foil or 2 paper bags
- Special things to put inside, like glitter, stars, confetti, fabric shapes, lace, ribbon, foil strips, sequins, flowers, and leaves
- Iron
- Scissors
- Ribbon

IMAGINATION JOURNAL

WHAT YOU NEED

- Pressed flowers, leaves, or small household items like buttons, beads, sequins, etc.
- Blank journal or bound book, or several pages tied together with a pretty ribbon. (Use a hole puncher to make a hole in the top left corner of each page.)
- Tacky glue
- Crayons, markers, watercolors, or pens
- Drawings, photographs, or cut-out magazine pictures

Make a journal or diary for yourself or for someone really special. Write down your thoughts, ideas, experiences, or anything else! You can also paste in pictures of friends and family members and present it to them as a memory book.

WHAT YOU DO

1. Arrange flowers and other items on the front cover of your journal to make a nice design and then glue them on securely.
2. Write a title or word design on the front cover with your pens, markers, or crayons.
3. Use your imagination to write a creative story. Illustrate it with your own drawings, or glue in photos or pictures cut out from a magazine.

OTHER IDEAS

Take pictures of your favorite dolls, toys, friends, or places and glue them in your journal. Be sure to write their names, or you might forget many years later.

FOOD PAINT

Fairies always use natural material like vegetables, berries, and spices to make their own paint. You can, too! Use them for just about any arts and crafts project you want. They will last for a few days if you store them in your refrigerator. The paints may smell delicious, but please don't taste them!

All your dreams can take flight at the twinkling of first star light!

WHAT YOU DO

- **Cocoa**—Mix a spoonful of cocoa with a few drops of water to make a nice muddy-brown paint.
- **Red currants, raspberries, or blackberries**—Take fresh or frozen berries and drop them into a blender with a little water to make some lovely colors.
- **Mustard**—Thin it with a few drops of water and you have a beautiful yellow paint.
- **Beets**—Put sliced raw, cooked, or canned beets into a blender with a few drops of water and mix. You'll get a deep pink color.
- **Powdered drink mix**—Beat an egg yolk and stir in a teaspoon of lemon-, orange-, or cherry-flavored powdered drink mix for a brightly colored paint.
- **Curry**—Mix a teaspoon of curry with water for a speckled reddish-orange.

NATURE WREATH

WHAT YOU NEED

- Pencil
- Thick piece of card-board
- Large or small paper plate
- Bowl or large cup
- Scissors
- Dried flowers, pinecones, nuts, seeds, pods, dried leaves, dried fruit
- Tacky glue
- String or thin wire
- Clear sealer or gloss enamel (optional)
- Ribbon

You can use practically anything you find to make a wreath. Besides being hung on the wall, a wreath also makes a great centerpiece on a table.

WHAT YOU DO

1. Trace a circle onto the cardboard, using the paper plate as your outline. Use a bowl or a large cup as a pattern for the hole in the middle of the wreath. Cut around the outer edge of the wreath and then cut out the hole in the middle.
2. Glue lots of dried flowers and other natural things to the cardboard. Allow to dry overnight.
3. Use string or wire to attach anything large or heavy like dried fruit or pinecones.
4. You can spray your wreath with a clear sealer or gloss enamel to make it last longer.
5. Hang your wreath with a pretty ribbon tied at the top.

OTHER IDEAS

- **Spice wreath**—Glue cardamom pods, peppercorns, bay leaves, cloves, star anise, and cinnamon sticks to the cardboard.
- **Herbal wreath**—Glue on large or whole pieces of dried herbs like rosemary, thyme, oregano, marjoram, bayberries, and chive blossoms.
- **Play-Doh wreath**—Use baked Play-Doh cut into different cookie shapes to decorate the cardboard.
- **Friendly animal wreath**—Dry out the seed head from a sunflower. Use toothpicks or peanut butter to attach edible decorations, like birdseed and pieces of bread to it. Carefully stick a piece of wire through the sunflower head and hang it on a tree or fence for your neighborhood birds to eat. If you have a hamster, gerbil, mouse, or pet rat, you can put the wreath in their cage so they can have a little nibble!
- **Bird wreath**—You can also lightly spread bagel halves with peanut butter and sprinkle them with birdseed. For a special treat, string breakfast cereals into garlands and hang them on a tree. You can use a needle and thread, or you can just slide a string through any cereal with holes in the middle.

What did the tree say to the pixie?

Leaf me alone!!

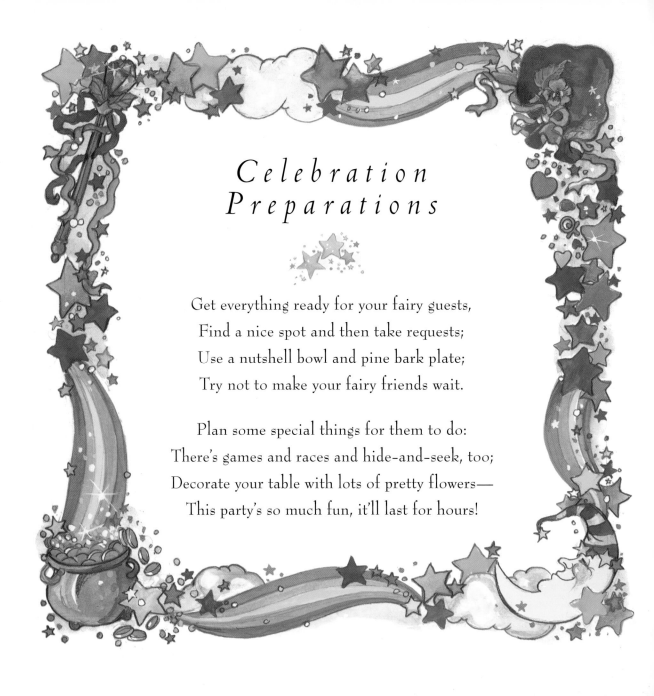

Celebration Preparations

Get everything ready for your fairy guests,
Find a nice spot and then take requests;
Use a nutshell bowl and pine bark plate;
Try not to make your fairy friends wait.

Plan some special things for them to do:
There's games and races and hide-and-seek, too;
Decorate your table with lots of pretty flowers—
This party's so much fun, it'll last for hours!

FAIRY SONGS

Songs are such fun to sing, especially at a party. You can sing a song you know or you can make up your own verses to melodies you know.

- Try this song to the tune of "If you're happy and you know it":

  If you are a friendly fairy, wave your wings,
  If you are a friendly fairy, wave your wings,
  If you are a friendly fairy,
  Then your life will be so merry,
  If you are a friendly fairy, wave your wings.

- You can play song games by having everyone sit in a circle and choosing one friend to name three silly words. Then have everyone sing a song to the tune of "The Farmer in the Dell." For example, if the player's three words are "pickles," "pigs," and "belly buttons," everyone would sing this:

  Pickles, pigs, and belly buttons,
  Pickles, pigs, and belly buttons,
  Heigh-ho the derry-oh,
  Pickles, pigs, and belly buttons.

Make up new verses for the song by letting everyone have a turn naming three silly words.

Always keep a song in your heart and a smile on your face!

FAIRY BIRTHDAY PARTY PICNIC

WHAT YOU NEED

- $8\frac{1}{2}$-by-11-inch sheets of paper, one per guest
- Envelopes at least 5 by 6 inches, one per guest
- Markers, crayons, colored pencils
- Glue
- Glitter, jewels, ribbons, lace, sequins, pressed flowers and leaves, stickers, rubber stamps

Springtime is when the fairies work their most powerful magic, helping flowers bloom. Even though most of their celebrations are held during the delightful month of May, you can plan a fairy birthday picnic on any nice sunny day.

FAIRY INVITATIONS

WHAT YOU DO

1. Fold each piece of paper in half lengthwise. Then fold it in half again (see the illustration).

2. Write your message on the front and inside of the invitation.
3. Glue your decorations onto the front and inside pages and let dry.

4. Address and stamp your envelopes first, then stick in the invitations. You can also decorate the outside of the envelopes.

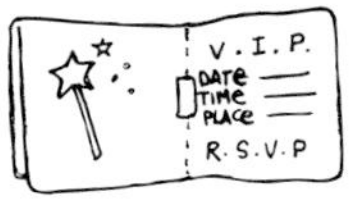

5. Be sure to mail your invitations at least two weeks in advance so that your guests can make plans for your party.

MAGIC DECORATIONS

WHAT YOU DO

1. Cover your table (or the ground) with a pretty tablecloth. You can also glue things like glitter or pretty pictures onto an old fabric or paper tablecloth.
2. If you have any fairy, troll, sprite, or elf dolls, be sure to display them as centerpieces.
3. Use your hands to scrunch up a few feet of tulle and place it so that it winds around the table.
4. Cut pieces of ribbon or crepe paper 1 to 2 feet long. Let a grown-up curl the ribbon by pulling it between their thumb and the blade of a pair of scissors. Twist the crepe paper. Scatter the ribbon or crepe paper curls around the table; if it's a windy day, you may want to tape them down.
5. Be sure to sprinkle some flowers and Fairy Dust on top of your table.
6. If you have balloons, carefully glue glitter or any other sparkly things on them. Use curling ribbon to tie the balloons to your table, chairs, or nearby trees.

WHAT YOU NEED

- A tablecloth big enough to cover your table or the ground where your guests will be sitting
- Tacky glue
- Glitter, sequins, pictures, etc.
- Fairy dolls or other pretty things for a centerpiece
- A few feet of netting (tulle)
- Curling ribbon or crepe paper
- Scissors
- Scotch tape (optional)
- Flowers and Fairy Dust (see page 10)
- Balloons

FAIRY FOOD

WHAT YOU NEED

- Two $1\frac{1}{2}$-liter bottles raspberry ginger ale
- $\frac{1}{2}$ pint fresh strawberries
- Fresh, clean mint leaves

Make some delicious Famous Fairy Cakes and serve Pixie Power Punch at your party. The fairies' original recipe for this punch was to blend sweet drops of spring rain and early morning dew, and then add the nectar of violets. Since it may be hard for you to gather those ingredients, just go to your grocery store! Make sure to have a grown-up help you when cooking!

PIXIE POWER PUNCH

WHAT YOU DO

1. Chill the ginger ale and pour it into a punch bowl or pitcher.
2. Hull and slice the strawberries and drop them into the ginger ale.
3. Decorate with sprigs of mint. Sip and dream.

This serves up to ten fairy friends.

FAMOUS FAIRY CAKES

WHAT YOU DO

1. Crack the eggs into one bowl.
2. With the electric mixer, beat them until thick and fluffy. Slowly add the sugar and beat well.
3. Beat in the milk and vanilla.
4. In the other bowl, mix together the flour, baking powder, and salt. Add to the egg mixture and beat until smooth.
5. Spread the batter in a greased and floured jelly roll pan.
6. Bake at 375 degrees for 12 to 15 minutes. When cool, cut the cake using a small biscuit cutter or different-shaped cookie cutters.
7. Decorate with Rainbow Cake Frosting and candy sprinkles.

This recipe makes 6 to 8 small round or square fairy cakes.

THINGS YOU NEED

- 2 bowls
- Electric mixer
- Spoon
- Jelly roll pan (cookie sheet), $12\frac{1}{2}$ by $10\frac{1}{2}$ inches
- Biscuit cutter or cookie cutters

FOODS YOU NEED

- 3 large eggs (at room temperature)
- 1 cup sugar
- 5 tablespoons milk
- $1\frac{1}{2}$ teaspoons vanilla
- 1 cup flour
- 1 teaspoon baking powder
- $\frac{1}{4}$ teaspoon salt
- Candy sprinkles

RAINBOW CAKE FROSTING

THINGS YOU NEED

- Large bowl
- 4 small bowls
- Pastry bags and decorating tips (optional)
- Spoons and knives
- Very Special Edible Magic (see page 69)

FOODS YOU NEED

- 1 stick butter, left at room temperature until soft
- ¾ cup powdered sugar
- ¾ teaspoon of your favorite flavor extract—vanilla, strawberry, etc.
- ¼ cup milk
- Red, yellow, blue, and green food coloring

WHAT YOU DO

1. Mix the softened butter and the sugar together in the large bowl. Add the flavor extract and a little milk for a good frosting texture.
2. Divide the frosting into the four small bowls. Add a drop of red food coloring to the first bowl, a drop of yellow coloring to the second bowl, a drop of blue to the third bowl, and a drop of green to the fourth. Mix each one well with a clean spoon.
3. Fill the pastry bag with one of the colored frostings, and use a different tip with each color to decorate your Famous Fairy Cakes. Clean the pastry bag and repeat with other colors. Or use spoons and knives to create lovely patterns.
4. Decorate the cakes with Very Special Edible Magic.

This will be enough frosting for 6 to 8 small fairy cakes.

VERY SPECIAL EDIBLE MAGIC

You can decorate cakes, cupcakes, or cookies by dipping or sprinkling them with any of these tasty treats:

Powdered sugar ♥ Cinnamon ♥ Coconut flakes
Raisins ♥ Cookie & cracker crumbs ♥ Nuts
Sesame seeds ♥ Mini marshmallows ♥ Nutmeg
Dried fruit ♥ Colored sprinkles ♥ Colored sugar
Chocolate chips ♥ Poppy seeds ♥ Pomegranate seeds

WISHING ON A BIRTHDAY CAKE

Everybody knows that to make a wish, you must blow out all the candles on your birthday cake. What people don't know is that if you don't blow out all your candles at once, you'll still get your wish. You'll just have to wait a bit longer. If you don't want to take any chances, try this wish on your fairy birthday cake:

Birthday cake, birthday cake,
Please grant me every wish I make;
If I don't blow out every flame,
Please answer my wishes all the same!

Knock, knock!
Who's there?
Arthur.
Arthur who?
Arthur (are there) any fairy cakes left?

FUN AND GAMES

Did you hear
the joke about the
cloud?
*Never mind. It's way over
your head!*

Fairies love to play fun games with their friends. Here are some of their favorites.

GUESS WHAT I AM?

What's fluffy white and floats up high,
Like piles of ice cream in the sky?

What's a red, green, or golden fruit
That grows from trees with very deep roots?

Most folks get a rash when I am around;
I make them itch if they pick me off the ground.

I am many colors outside and inside,
and from sun and rain I cannot hide.

I am a female bug with wings;
I'm one of the beetles, but I don't sting.

ANSWERS

1. clouds 2. apple 3. poison ivy 4. rainbow
5. ladybug

TWO FAIRY TONGUE TWISTERS

How many times can you say these two Fairy Tongue Twisters as fast as you can?

Twelve Tall Tulips Turning to the Tree

You have no need to light a night-light on a light night like tonight, for a night-light lights a slight light, and tonight's a night that's light. When a night's light, like tonight's light, it's really not quite right to light night-lights with their slight lights, on a light night like tonight.

TAKE-TEN TRICK

This easy but tricky trick is sure to make your friends laugh. Take nine sticks or twigs or branches, count them out loud, and lay them in a bundle on the ground. Tell your audience that you are going to turn those nine sticks into TEN by magic, without breaking them. Wave your magic wand and say a few magic words. Then simply take the nine sticks and lay them out to spell the word *TEN.* This trick fools them every time!

Here are some special rhymes to say when you use your wand to perform a trick:

"Hocus-pocus, on this trick, please focus."

Or

"Fairy friends old and new, please make this magic trick come true."

FAIRY TREE

WHAT YOU NEED

- Coffee or other large can
- Sand
- Small or medium-sized fallen tree branch (no longer than 2 feet) with many little branches
- Thread, string, ribbon, or yarn
- Things to decorate with, like pinecones, feathers, dried flowers, leaves, etc.
- Glue
- Glitter

Fairies love to decorate their trees with ornaments that they've found nearby.

WHAT YOU DO

1. Fill the coffee can with sand. This will help your "tree" stand straight up and not tip over.
2. Remove the leaves from the little branches, then stick the branches into the sand.
3. Decorate your fairy tree with feathers, flowers, pinecones, etc., by tying them onto the little branches with yarn, string, thread, or ribbon. Dab a little glue on the tree and sprinkle some glitter to make it more magical.

OTHER IDEAS

- **Candy tree**—Attach different colored hard candies on the branches with glue or ribbon.
- **Framed picture tree**—Gather photos of your family and friends or cut out colorful pictures from magazines. Frame them with colored pipe cleaners by gluing the pipe cleaners onto the edge of the pictures. Tie a piece of ribbon into a loop and glue onto the back of the picture. When completely dried, tie onto the branches with some fancy bows. Or you can just tape some favorite pictures to the tree.

CRAZY KALEIDOSCOPE

Look through a Fairy Kaleidoscope and you will see a world that is bright and beautiful.

WHAT YOU DO

1. Slide the sheet of silver Mylar paper into the empty paper towel tube.
2. Put a dot of glue on the back side of the Mylar near both ends of the tube. This way, the Mylar will stick to the tube and not move around.
3. Holding the tube upright, place one 6-inch piece of clear plastic wrap across the top end of the tube, and then carefully place a little glitter, seeds, confetti, even a drop of vegetable oil on the plastic wrap.
4. Cover with the second piece of plastic wrap and tightly secure both layers with a rubber band.
5. Aim the covered end at a sunny window and look through the open end while slowly turning the tube. Doesn't it seem as if you've just entered fairyland?

WHAT YOU NEED

- Sheet of silver Mylar paper
- Empty paper towel roll
- Glue
- Two 6-inch pieces of clear plastic wrap
- Glitter, seeds, confetti
- Vegetable oil (optional)
- Rubber band

FAIRY TELESCOPE

WHAT YOU NEED

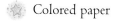

- Colored paper
- Scissors
- Empty tube from a paper towel or toilet paper roll
- Crayons, markers, or stickers
- Glue or tape
- String or yarn

Finding fairies is easy if you are wearing a Fairy Telescope around your neck. It will also help you to spot a fancy flower, an unusual tree, or little bugs and animal friends.

WHAT YOU DO

1. Cut a piece of colored paper so that it fits completely around your empty tube.
2. Decorate the colored paper with crayons, markers, or stickers and let it dry.
3. Glue or tape the decorated paper to the tube, leaving the ends of the tube open.
4. Poke two holes near one end of the roll. Thread some string or yarn through the holes and make a necklace-sized loop. Tie off the loop with a knot. Now you can wear the Fairy Telescope around your neck.

MAGICAL STONES

Fairies love pretty stones, and you can make your own.

WHAT YOU DO

1. Wash and dry all your stones.
2. Use your pencil to sketch designs, pictures, and words like "Believe," "Love," "Imagine," "Dream," or a name on the stones.

3. Then use your paint to color in your pencil drawings. While the paint is still wet, sprinkle on the glitter.
4. When the paint is dry, glue on your other decorations. You can use your Magical Stones as paperweights, doorstops, decorations, and inspirations.

WHAT YOU NEED

- Smooth stones
- Pencil
- Tempera paints
- Paintbrush
- Cup of water (for rinsing your brush)
- Glitter
- Decorations like sequins, crystals, gemstones, etc.
- Tacky glue

BUILDING A FAIRY NEST

WHAT YOU NEED

- Clay or Play-Doh
- Leaves, twigs, grasses, feathers, yarn, fabric, etc.

Like birds, fairies use practically anything found in nature to build their nests. You, too, can build a nest.

WHAT YOU DO

1. Roll a piece of clay or Play-Doh into a ball about the size of your palm.
2. Stick your thumb into the center of the clay ball to create a smooth "nest."
3. As you walk, look for things to add to your nest, like twigs, dry grasses, fallen leaves, pine needles, bits of bark, or feathers. You can also squish in little pieces of colored yarn, string, or scraps of fabric found around your home. Keep adding to your nest until you feel it is ready for a homeless winged creature.
4. Place your nest on a tree branch or in a big shrub where birds can easily discover it. If you can, check every now and then (very quietly) to see if a bird or fairy has decided to use your nest.

FISHING FOR FAIRIES

Anyone can try to catch fishes, but how many people can catch a fairy?

WHAT YOU DO

1. Draw and cut out several cardboard or construction paper fairies (see the pattern).

2. Slide a paper clip around the middle of each fairy and place them all in a shallow bowl. If you want, you can decorate the bowl with flowers and plants.

3. Use string or thick thread to tie a small household magnet to the end of a pencil. Drop your pole into the bowl of paper fairies. Whoever catches the most fairies wins! You can make the game more interesting by using a blindfold.

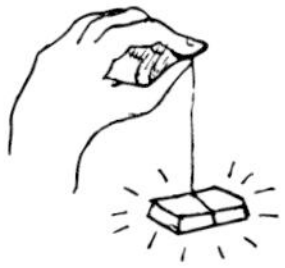

OTHER IDEAS

- You can use the same pattern to make a flying fairy mobile, by using tissue paper instead of cardboard. Tape a piece of thread to each fairy's back and tie them to a clothes hanger. Hang the hanger near a window, and the slightest breeze will send your fairies fluttering.

WHAT YOU NEED

- Cardboard or colored construction paper
- Pencils
- Scissors
- Paper clips
- Shallow bowl
- Flowers or plants (optional)
- String or thick thread
- Small magnet

MAKING MUSICAL INSTRUMENTS

WHAT YOU NEED

- Cans, pans, bowls, boxes, bottles, etc.
- Wax paper or thick plastic
- Rubber band

Listening to music is so easy because it's everywhere—just open your ears! All the sounds of nature are like music to a fairy's ears. Making your own music is just as simple.

WHAT YOU DO

- If you want to feel the rhythm, simply tap a beat on your knees or snap your fingers.
- You can also bang on empty plastic bottles or shake gravel-filled soup cans.
- Make drums by using pans, plastic bowls, empty boxes, or cans with their tops covered with wax paper or thick plastic, pulled tight and smooth and held in place by a thick rubber band.
- Make neat horn sounds by blowing across and down into an empty glass or plastic bottle. Put your bottom lip up against the near edge of the hole, push your upper lip out a little, and over the top of the hole. Make an O shape with your lips, and then blow out a steady stream of air.

WATER MUSIC

WHAT YOU DO

- To design your own fairy sounds, pour water into four or five glasses of water. Fill up each glass to a different level to create different tones. Add a drop of food coloring and a flower to each one to create a pretty rainbow effect. Gently tap the glasses with a spoon to play some delightful music.
- You can also hold your water glass at the bottom with one hand (to keep it from tipping over) and with the wet index finger of your other hand, lightly rub the glass rim. Don't press hard; just keep the pressure even. You'll hear a high-pitched hum from the glass that will increase with the pressure and speed of your finger. You will have to stop every so often to rewet your finger or the hum will stop.

WHAT YOU NEED

- Glasses
- Water
- Food coloring (optional)
- Flowers (optional)
- Spoon

A fairy's laugh is like music—it lingers in your heart!

CLAPPERS AND WHISTLES

WHAT YOU DO

- Create clappers by taking two spoons and holding them so that their rounded parts face each other. One spoon should rest between your thumb and the knuckle of your first finger. The other spoon will rest between your first and second fingers. Then, tap them against your thigh or palm so that they smack each other.

- Great whistles can be made from small leaves or pieces of grass. Any leaf that is at least 1 inch long and not more than ½ inch wide is fine. Hold your thumbs side by side, with the blade of grass flat between your thumb knuckles. Then cup your hands and bend your thumb tops over them. Blow through your thumb knuckles and the grass.

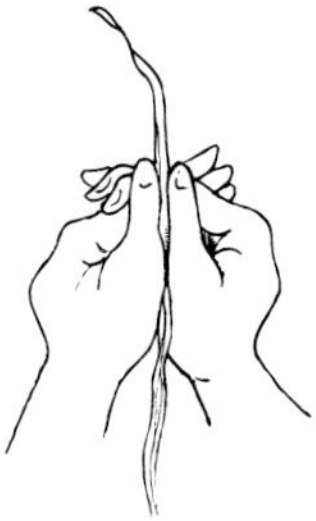

FAIRY TWO-STEP

Fairies absolutely love to dance. They do it every chance they get. This is a great dance to do by yourself or with a group of fairy friends. It's kind of like an Irish jig, but you can use any lively music for dancing.

WHAT YOU DO

1. Place a flower on the ground in front of you so that you can dance around it.
2. Start with your hands on your hips, or else hold hands with your fairy friends.
3. With your knee bent to the sky, kick your right leg up so that the inside of your heel points upward to the sky.
4. Set it back down and kick up your left leg, with your heel pointing upward.
5. After you kick your right leg and your left, raise your arms up and down as if you were flying. Flap your wings four times as you skip around the flower.
6. Keep raising up your right foot, then your left foot, and flapping your "wings" as you and your friends dance around the flower. Before you know it, you will feel like a real fairy!

Rainbow Friendship Wish

Fairy Friend so fair and bright,
Come and be my chosen sprite;
When I reach the rainbow's end,
The gold I'll give to you, my friend;
I'll keep the colors and their hues—
Red, green, yellow, purple, and blue.

SECRET MESSAGES

Here's how you can send a secret message to a friend.

WHAT YOU DO

1. Dissolve 1 tablespoon sugar in ½ cup water, lemon juice, or milk.
2. Dip a paintbrush in your magical solution and write your note on a piece of paper.
3. When the message dries, the words will be invisible, but when your friend has a grown-up press the paper with a warm iron, your secret words will come back like magic!

WHAT YOU NEED

- Sugar
- Water, lemon juice, or milk
- Paintbrush
- Paper
- Iron

CATCHING FIREFLIES

WHAT YOU NEED

- Glass jar
- Piece of paper
- Rubber band
- Toothpick

When the sun goes down and the stars come out, the fairy fun begins! You'll have lots of fun creating a firefly lantern to light the night sky.

WHAT YOU DO

1. Catch the fireflies or "lightning bugs" gently with your hands and release them into a glass jar.
2. Cover the jar opening with a sheet of paper and secure it with a rubber band.
3. Carefully poke a few tiny holes in the paper cover with a toothpick and you've created your very own twinkling lamp.
4. When you are ready to go to bed, be sure to set your fireflies free so they can light the way for a wandering fairy friend.

MOONLIGHTING MOTHS

Moths and fireflies are distant cousins of fairies because they're on the wing all through the night. Here's a magical way to attract moths.

WHAT YOU DO

1. Heat ¼ cup sugar and 1 cup water in a saucepan until the sugar is dissolved. (Have a grown-up help you!)
2. With a paintbrush, paint the side of a tree or an outside wall with the cooled sugar water just before night falls.
3. Take your flashlight and visit the tree later in the evening. Have you ever seen so many moths before? Count how many moths you see.

WHAT YOU NEED

- ¼ cup sugar
- 1 cup water
- Saucepan
- Paintbrush
- Flashlight

FLASHLIGHT FUN

If you turn on the light suddenly at night, you might catch fairy folk dancing!

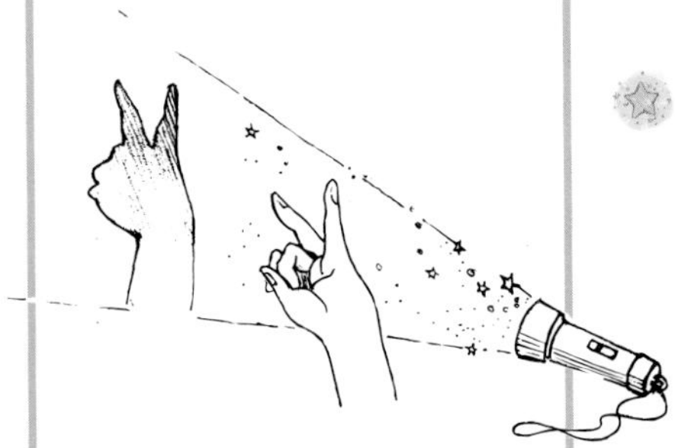

Here are some fairy ways to have fun with your friends after dark.

WHAT YOU DO

- Inside your room, turn off the lights and turn on your flashlight. Make a spooky face by holding your flashlight under your chin so that the light shines up on your face. The shadows on your face might scare even you if you look into the mirror.
- You can make shadow puppets with your hands. If you make a fist with two fingers in a V shape and hold it in front of the flashlight beam, you'll see a rabbit's head appear on the wall. Move it and it looks like it's hopping. Have a friend hold the flashlight, then place your two hands next to each other with your fingers spread out and your thumbs crossing. This will make a bird or fairy. Flap your hands to get it to fly.
- You can cut lots of little holes in a paper bag and shine the flashlight through the bag to see the "stars" it creates. Try cutting out your initials or some other interesting shapes. Or make your own planetarium from a cleaned-out milk carton. Just cut off the top section and poke holes in the bottom with a pin. Place a flashlight inside and aim your planetarium at a dark ceiling in your room. Do you see any starlight formations?

FAIRY GLITTER DOME

A glitter dome is a way to create your very own miniature fairyland.

WHAT YOU DO

1. Add a tablespoon of glitter and/or confetti to the glass jar.
2. Fill the jar with water almost to the top.
3. Add food coloring or small toys.
4. Put a small amount of glue on the inside of the jar lid and close the jar tightly.
5. When the lid is dry, shake your magical fairy dome to make it come to life.

WHAT YOU NEED

- Clean baby food jar or other small glass jar, labels removed
- Glitter and/or Mylar confetti
- Water
- Drop of food coloring (optional)
- Tiny plastic toys (optional)
- Glue

RAISING A RAINBOW

WHAT YOU NEED

- Clear glass of water
- A table
- White poster board or index card
- Flashlight

Did you know you can create a rainbow after dark? It's true, if you follow these fairy easy steps.

WHAT YOU DO

1. Fill a clear glass with water and set it near the edge of a table in a room that you can make dark.
2. Prop up a piece of white poster board or an index card on the table, about 3 inches away from the glass.
3. Darken the room.
4. Then shine a flashlight so that the beam hits the edge of the table and angles through the glass.
5. Adjust the position of the flashlight until a rainbow appears on the paper.

FAIRY'S S'MORES

End a great day with a delicious good-night treat of Fairy's S'mores.

WHAT YOU NEED

- 2 marshmallows
- Candy sprinkles
- Piece of a chocolate bar
- 2 graham-cracker squares
- Aluminum foil

WHAT YOU DO

1. Place two marshmallows, candy sprinkles, and a piece of a chocolate bar between two graham-cracker squares.
2. Wrap each "sandwich" in aluminum foil.
3. Bake in a 275-degree oven for five minutes, or wrap in a paper towel and microwave for one minute. Yummy on the tummy!

Flying with Fairies

It's so wonderful to be outside,
To swing on daisies and daffodil slides;
Of all the enchanted games to play,
Which are the ones you'll choose today?

Climb an oak or weeping willow,
Fly to the moon and land on your pillow;
Make believe and let's pretend—
Tell a secret to your fairy friend!

Float like a leaf or like a feather,
Fairies fly in any weather;
We whirl and twirl and dance around,
For it is joy that we have found.

THE FAIRY DUST CLUB

Would you like to join the newest, most magical club around? Just fill out the form below and you will receive a special Fairy Dust Club membership package containing:

- Official Fairy Dust Club Membership Card and Certificate
- Magic Fairy Dust
- Fairy Dust Club Pin
- Fairy Dust Club Newsletter listing fun projects, activities, crafts, and games that have been created for you, your home, school, community, and planet. Fairy Dust Club members will also be able to share any special wishes, silly spells and chants, fairy thoughts or messages.

To join, simply fill out the section below and mail it with a check or money order for $5.00 (U.S.)/ $7.50 (Canada) (to cover the costs of materials, printing, shipping & handling) to: Fairy Dust Club, 927 Country Valley Road, Westlake Village, CA 91362

Cut here

Name: ______________________________ Age: ____ Girl [ ] Boy [ ]
Address: ____
City: ____________________ State: __________ Zip Code: ________
Birthday: ________________________
Special wish, spell, message, or thought: ___________________________

____

A word about the Fairy Fund: This private nonprofit organization located in Westlake Village, California, donates a portion of this book's proceeds to groups directly benefiting needy children across the United States and internationally. The Fairy Fund also accepts donations from individuals and corporations.

ACKNOWLEDGMENTS

I count myself as being truly blessed for having met so many wonderful people throughout my life. Their love, guidance, and kindness have given me tremendous fairy faith that has enabled me to write this book. I would like to give thanks to each and every one of them as well as special thanks to the following people:

- All the fairy doll makers, craft artisans, authors, researchers, philosophers, and, of course, the many fairies who have inspired me with their thoughts, teachings, and creations. A special thanks to Betsy Williams for her delicious fairy cake and punch recipes.
- My literary agents, Meredith Bernstein and Elizabeth Cavanaugh, for recognizing a "charming" book concept and helping me to navigate it through frequently rough seas.
- My editor, Annetta Hanna at Clarkson Potter, for her ability to quickly visualize my book's direction and stay on top of it through final publication.
- My art director, Marysarah Quinn, for her wonderful enthusiasm and attentiveness. Her artistic sense is only surpassed by her kindness.
- My illustrator, Linda Cohen, for her delightful illustrations. I am indeed fortunate to have such a talented artist enter my Maginary Way.
- The very talented Lydia Halverson and her agent, Gayle Crump McNeil, for their understanding nature.
- My dearest fairy friends (and you know who you are), who for years have always listened

to my hopes and wishes and encouraged me to keep on dreaming. You are all, without a doubt, the beautiful blossoms of my life.

- My brothers, Frank and Bruce, for their quiet support and not-so-quiet teasing about fairies.

- My creative twin sister, Lori, who came up with some wonderful games and crafts for my book. I always knew you were a fairy at heart. Your love and support mean so much to me!

- My very imaginative son, Brendan (who is still learning to live The Fairy Way), for his wonderful fairy stories that make me laugh till I cry. You are so precious!

- My multitalented daughter, Lindsey (who is the true essence of a fairy), for not only listening to my fairy philosophies but for helping me to create new fairy characters, poems, stories, and pictures. You are pure goodness!

- My husband, Arnie, for co-supporting my fairy doll habit, understanding my feelings, giving me the room I needed to grow, for remaining open to all possibilities, and for taking the time to learn about New Age theories. I love you and appreciate you more as the years pass by us.

- Last and certainly most important, my mom, who not only helped me with my book but taught me how to use my imagination when I was just a wee little fairy. You always believed in me. I owe you all the joy and happiness I have ever experienced. My heart-light is yours!

INDEX

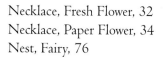